ROOSEVELT ETHRIDGE

I0191445

THE MAKING OF A *Prayer* WARRIOR

ESSENTIALS FOR GROWTH IN PRAYER

CREATION
HOUSE

The Making of a Prayer Warrior
by Roosevelt Ethridge, Jr.
Published by Creation House
A Charisma Media Company
600 Rinehart Road
Lake Mary, Florida 32746
www.charismamedia.com

Unless otherwise noted, all Scripture quotations are from the King James Version of the Bible.

Scripture quotations marked NKJV are taken from the New King James Version®. Copyright © 1982 by Thomas Nelson. Used by permission. All rights reserved.

Cover design by Kimberly R. Walston for Pages Design Studio

Back cover author photo by Michael Herring for Michael Herring Photography

Visit the author's website: reliveglobal.org.

International Standard Book Number: 978-1-62999-231-0
E-book International Standard Book Number: 978-1-62999-232-7

While the author has made every effort to provide accurate telephone numbers and Internet addresses at the time of publication, neither the publisher nor the author assumes any responsibility for errors or for changes that occur after publication.

First edition

18 19 20 21 22 — 987654321
Printed in the United States of America

This work is in honor of the late Reverend Roosevelt Ethridge, Sr.

The mantle of prayer that was deposited onto me from birth has been amazing. I am forever grateful for the image of prayer that you presented before me. The prayer warrior you were has forever embedded in my life a hunger and passion for prayer. Blessings, from the legacy that you left and from others' practice, endure. Your life of a prayer warrior abides on in the lives of those of us who continue to walk in prayer. I am forever grateful, your son.

This book is birthed from a place of adversity. I dedicate it to those who have witnessed my perseverance in life. The prayers of the righteous have been an overwhelming blessing to me.

Being raised in a house of prayer has imparted a positive response to prayer within my life.

CONTENTS

CONTENTS

INTRODUCTION

―――――――

PRAYER IS AN important factor in every aspect of humanity and society. Prayer is so readily used that we frequently fail to observe how often this discipline is practiced in everyday life. Prayer is used in meetings, sports, hospitals, government, and church. Every religion has a form of prayer. Even atheists pray. Communion with deities is important in every religion because access to them is often through prayer.

Prayer time with God should exude the power of His glory and verify His majestic omnipresence. Spending time with God multiplies His Spirit within us. Prayer is man's right to access the Father while being an instrument of His glory.

Prayer changes character and perception. How we have been taught to see things can either help us or hinder us from seeing the fruit and/or evidence of prayer. It is not uncommon for people to conduct prayer out of their immaturity. Culture and community can subliminally teach us appropriate ways to petition God, but these early disciplines of prayer are known to develop and change over the course of time.

Intercessors and people of prayer must develop prayer through practice. "Real prayer is something we learn."[1] However, philosophies and traditions have created diversity in basic disciplines. Many people consider what they know about prayer to be enough. Often, they search for teaching in areas of life and ministry other than prayer. Those who are taught during adolescent years will require apprenticeship in prayer as they grow in spirit and faith.

Identity and familiarity in prayer should not be depreciated by lack of character or difficulty in worship. "Worship is about God—and God is not for sale, not a commodity to be marketed like aspirin through either 'high' or 'low' church services."[2]

The twenty-first-century church has become lax in enforcing disciplines that should be practiced by intercessors. Though some people boast of their time spent with God, this boasting is not displaying the greater characteristics of God that should be readily evident in the life of an intercessor. Our character is often times on display for observation and critique. Character is a major part of our role in developing intimacy with the Father. Character is connected to integrity.

Once I was asked, "Why is character so important if anyone can pray?"

The question ignited a flame in me to address their concern. I provided the individual with a scenario: "Suppose you or a family member was terminally ill, and you were accustomed to asking someone in your church or a family member that seemed to be devoted to God to pray for a miracle healing to happen. So, they agreed to your request. Two weeks went by after the prayer, and you ran into this individual at the beauty salon. You noticed the individual using vain language such as swearing, cursing, and other blasphemous actions and also mocking your request for agreement in prayer. Or, what if you overheard that individual openly display their lack of self-control by telling about enjoying sex with a lover the previous evening? How would you evaluate the respect you have for that individual?"

Their response was, "I would feel somewhat betrayed, and I would probably never go to them again and ask for them to touch and agree with me in prayer."

If we possess God-like character, then we are more certain of who we are and whose we are. If we know whose we are as intercessors, then we will be more conscious of the decisions we make in governing our lives.

Many prayer ministries and teams overlook character as being one of the foundational principles for governing and operating in prayer. Prayer ministry teams are attractive, and every ministry feels it must have one. However, we must not get caught in the whirlwind of just putting anyone in place to spearhead this ministry. People are vulnerable when interacting with the prayer ministry team or persons. So, as leaders, we must be prayerful and watchful of the management of this ministry. We mustn't choose just anyone; we must let their lives speak of their ability to qualify. Prayer can be engaged by anyone, but for prayer warriors, there are needed stages of growth that must be acknowledged. There are foundational values of which every prayer warrior should have knowledge:

- How long has prayer been in existence?
- What is prayer?
- Are prayer and meditation the same thing?
- Forms of prayer

Prayer has been in existence since the beginning of time; God activated the governing "laws of prayer" when He spoke in Genesis 1:26. He said, "Let us make man...." This was the first verification of our deity summoning Himself to produce something; He understood the power of prayer. We are living in a time where many people don't know what prayer is, and this hinders their ability to engage it.

Prayer is:

a. Communion with God

b. Petition made to a deity

c. The intercourse of the soul with God[3]

Meditation and prayer are not the same thing. Though people may get these two actions mixed up because both put us into a quiet state of mind, they are distinctively different. To meditate is to reflect on or contemplate. We meditate on scripture to boost our faith in God's ability to do what we've petitioned Him to do. Meditation is a tool that can be practiced, and it will produce encouragement and an increase in knowledge. Great thinkers often meditate to help produce new information and theories. The great Martin Luther practiced meditation. Also, Paul, John, David, Solomon—all in the Bible—practiced meditation.

Prayer, however, puts us in a place of looking for God. Different religions have different forms of prayer, such as some allowing only leaders to pray. Muslims pray dedicatedly three times a day. This is not a common discipline across the board for Christians. It is more common for us to pray out of need than to pray out of a sense of duty. In America, we involve prayer in more areas of life than other countries and religions. Even though many Americans include prayer in their lives, there are many who do not even believe in God.

Every intercessor needs to know the two forms of prayer: social and personal. It is not uncommon for people to be asked to perform acts of prayer for social occasions. Knowing the forms of prayer helps the intercessor to articulate and specify the prayer for directed purposes.

Social prayer

Social prayers are usually specific to a place and time. They are used in family prayers, worship services, public activities, etc. Corporate settings that involve more than one person are an environment for social prayers. Often prayer ministry leaders, pastors, reverends, and the like lead social prayers. Social prayers are highly respected and demanded. In most settings, people favor beginning their agendas with prayer. This is not restricted or limited to civic duties, sports, worship services, surgery, etc.

Currently in our country, the area where prayer is often challenged dearly is in public school. That is due to the increasing population composed of many different ethnicities and cultures. The government is becoming increasingly concerned about not offending others or being "politically correct" more than focusing on staying true to the constitution. It is often not the prayer that is causing the offense but has more to do with belief in God. America is being forced toward proclaiming that it has no belief in a God, and this is atheism. The Bible refers to this attitude as that of the Antichrist.

However, even with the hindrances from legislation in regards to prayer, there is still much room for prayer in society. Social prayers differ greatly from that of personal prayer.

Personal prayer

Personal prayer consists of personal time with God; mindfulness of prayers offered in social gatherings; and the practice of humility, humbleness, forgiveness, and thankfulness in prayer. We cannot equate time spent in prayer to time that we spend building relationships, social communities, or careers. Time in prayer is timeless, because the results of prayer are timeless. As we grow in prayer, we will find ourselves devoting personal time to communicate with the Father. Purposely spending time with God develops a discipline that leads to always involving Him (the Father), even unconsciously. The more time we choose to spend with God, the greater our relationship develops with Him, including our prayer lives.

One of the qualities of an intercessor is a passion for development and experience. People who are close to God do not like to be ignorant towards God's ways! This means the closer we get to Him, the more we will desire to know Him. Then we will find ourselves learning of Him or hungering for the Word. Intercession cannot be developed without the Word of God as a foundation.

When Jesus gave the parable about the bridegroom, He was describing efforts to develop a foundational base for the disciples to see the benefit of having the Word with them. The posture of a prayer warrior desiring to understand God's divine power is associated with a praying leader. There are three areas of importance of which prayer warriors must be conscious:

1. Their accountability to prayer
2. Their motives for praying
3. Their character in prayer

Twenty-first-century prayer warriors have been accused of lacking discipline in their position as intercessors. Some who are not properly developed in character may imitate prayer warriors, though they seldom initiate prayer during spiritual warfare. Expectedly, they like the tangible emotional feelings and popularity that the image of a prayer warrior brings.

Just because a person has charisma or uses spiritual language does not guarantee they embody integrity or accountability to God. Leaders giving an account to God with continual and consistent devotion will develop character disciplines that will display His (God's) nature. Being accountable is being responsible, answerable, and explicable (capable of being explained).[4] Being accountable to God in prayer should inspire leaders with the ability to explain their behavior!

There are times when people don't understand charismatic ministry. The belief in the moving of the Holy Spirit who heals, speaks, and quickens has created a stigma in ministry. Statements such as, "We were led to do it," ("it" being embracing, praying, walking, running, shouting, etc.) have created prejudices, sometimes causing resistance to Pentecostal and charismatic driven ministries.

In the life of a prayer warrior, there will be God encounters that will cause one to move outside of his or her norms. The Holy Spirit provides confidence and boldness in times of need. "To understand that the work of prayer involves a learning process saves us from arrogantly dismissing it as false or unreal."[5] These things are understood when we have experienced spiritual growth and development in the things of God. God is not the author of confusion, and He is able to always provide understanding to prevent us judging or harshly critiquing things that are not easily understood. In 1 John 4:1–3, we read:

> Beloved, believe not every spirit, but try the spirits whether are of God: because many false prophets

are gone out into the world. Hereby know ye the Spirit of God: Every spirit that confesseth that Jesus Christ is come in the flesh is of God: And every spirit that confesseth not that Jesus Christ is come in the flesh is not of God: and this is that spirit of antichrist, whereof ye have heard that it should come; and even now already is it in the world.

In their application of this text, prayer warriors should not be rude or facetious. The intention of a prayer warrior is to bring peace and clarity where there is confusion. It is the nature of God to use people, at times, as a presence of light, bringing validity to His name and His work. However, a life commitment to prayer, meditation, and study brings creditability to the prayer warrior. This accountability should be a reminder of the active representation of God living in them by way of the Holy Spirit.

Accountability is progressive; in other words, with maturity comes greater accountability. Since we are accountable to God, then the failures of our flesh should eventually cease from hindering our experience with Him. As an example, we can look at Job 12:7–10 where Job was challenged to prove his accountability to God, which then authenticated his righteousness in God.

One attack on intercessors is when they are challenged in their dedication and commitment in communion with the Father (God). The Father (God) knows our responses and methodology in or towards situations. He waits to see if we are going to adhere to His will or promote our own will.

An intercessor should await a "rhema response" from God before handling or responding to any situation. A rhema response is God's answer to a problem, situation, or concern. This answer is customized to fit the current petition or situation. In these moments, a prayer warrior must possess patience and servitude. This will validate our dependability in God; where there is no dependability, there is no accountability. Accountability will strengthen our insight and understanding of trials and tribulations. "One of the most critical aspects in learning to pray for others is to get in contact with God so that His life and power can flow through us into others."[6]

As the prayer warrior within us continues to grow, the intercessor will notice God's pleasure with our growth and Satan's frustration with our growth. Below is a table illustrating the contrast of our maturity; Satan is never happy for our growth.

GOD'S GLORY	SATAN'S FRUSTRATION
Ensures our faith	We will be able to discern between the real voice of God and an impersonated voice of God.
Not bound by the weaknesses of our flesh	We will be able to discern the motives of the situation.
Validates our righteousness in Him (God)	We are not vulnerable to him (Satan).
Affirms and strengthens our recognition and hearing of God's voice.	We gain strength to encourage others that were victims of him and convince them to pursue God.
Enables us to walk in victory.	We become his enemy and not his prey.

When a person is devoted to prayer, they will develop a victorious attitude. Optimism is an attribute of prayer warriors. This does not denote that prayers warriors are absent of stress, pressure, or attitudes of defeat. In 1 Peter 5:10 it says, "But the God of all grace, who hath called us unto his eternal glory by Christ Jesus, after that ye have suffered a while, make you perfect, stablish, strengthen, settle you."[7]

With a victorious attitude, prayer warriors will find themselves living and managing a stress-free life and declaring the battle is won. Knowing that trials come to make us strong constitutes the embracing of trials rather than the rejection of them. Prayer warriors find development through adversity.

Intercessors should not manipulate people with spiritual gifts. Using spiritual gifts as a tool to draw people for selfish gain and to push personal agendas is dangerous. It is equally wrong to mislead them by alluding that God requires nothing of them. God is not the lottery! If we manage our accountability to Him, then we are conduits for His blessings. "Listening to God is the necessary prelude to intercession. The work of intercession, sometimes called the prayer of faith, presupposes that the prayer of guidance is perpetually ascending to the Father. We must hear, know, and obey the will of God before we pray it into the lives of others."[8] Prayer warriors can examine their motives by beginning with this series of personal questions:

1. When do I go to God?
2. How often do I talk to Him?
3. Does He have priority in my life?

After answering these questions, we should see a model overview of our motives for petitioning God as well as a prayer-life schematic. We must graduate from petitioning God only in emergencies and urgencies. As intercessors, we should devote time to prayer. Effectiveness is the overall thing that prayer warriors desire.

How does one gain power and effectiveness in prayer? Power in prayer does not come from praying loudly, or building large buildings, or purchasing large homes. In today's time, prayer power has been quantified by materialism. In the eyes of today's church, the size of our house, the quality of our car, and/or the massiveness of our ministry constitute power. Spiritual power is not established by economic status. Spiritual power is endowed by consistency of devotion and discipline to prayer.

As intercessors, our motives for praying in agreement with another person matter. We must also remember that intercessors are not root doctors, witches, or some type of magicians. In other words, we don't cast spells. We should not waver in our motives for prayer. In communicating with God, intercessors should not harbor selfish desires to entice others in the kingdom to entreat *them* as gods. We should practice routines of petitioning God for *His* will, not trying to bring Him to *our* will. In any situation, the "will" of the Father is the most important to desire. God's will is not bound or covenanted to our human pain, frustration, irritation, stress, fatigue, etc. The Word of God commits Him, faith in Him binds Him, and His commitment to His Word obligates Him. Intercessors must keep this knowledge in mind because this will always be true and can bring forth faith for manifestation.

A natural sign of spiritual maturity is the increased sensitivity in our natural senses. Our senses are governed by our flesh; however, they are brought to awareness by our brain. The Bible instructs believers to die to their flesh or put to death the deeds of their bodies (Rom. 8:13). Dying to the flesh does not mean death to our senses. Furthermore, if we kill the dominance of the flesh, then our spirit will override, and we will become more sensitive to the Spirit of God and in our senses. Carnally, it sounds like we are saying that we will taste better, hear better, see better, etc. No, we are alluding to the fact that if we kill the dominance of the flesh, then we will hear God better. We will see more results that look like God. We will become more in tune to His fragrance, and we will become more sensitive in His presence.

If we strengthen our senses in God, then we will eventually develop an awareness of Him when making decisions concerning our lives on earth. The more sensitive we become to the Father, the more assurance we have in our day-to-day living. Developing this characteristic will enhance our ability to recognize the glory, to become like an automatic faucet in sensing God's presence. This means we won't be waiting for His glory to come upon us; it will be more like becoming a greater witness of His glory being displayed in another vessel—ourselves. This is not to say we will walk error free. However, our sensitivity to God will equip us to identify our errors faster.

These are qualities that every intercessor should possess. These qualities accompany the code of conduct for interceding, as well as the guidelines for interceding. We are in the day where intercession is one of our greatest assets. Intercession will aid the kingdom as it catapults into the next dimension of earthly manifestation. Therefore, it is not healthy for children of the King to harbor fear in communicating with Him. This book provides tools for the believer to take hold of maturity without fear.

Chapter 1

THE INTERCESSOR

PRAYER IS ONE of the most widely publicized areas of spiritual need in ministry today, but it is a controversial topic. Many are distraught by the religious ideologies concerning prayer. Prayer is one of the most essential spiritual tools used in maintaining the course of Christian discipline. Therefore, this book supports the desire of Christians to mature and be groomed into true prayer warriors.

In today's church, prayer warriors are honored and held in great esteem. There is great respect for those who deny themselves normality in their lives in order to develop spirituality. A stardom-focused and celebrity-driven atmosphere has been created around them. They catch the attention of young people and saints who don't necessarily possess the needed spiritual gifts or talents to be selfless prayer warriors. It is tempting for them to desire to become understudies of these people in their local assemblies and try to duplicate the outward expressions and mannerisms in prayer without committing to the lifestyle that is displayed before them.

Prayer warriors are often revered but seldom celebrated for this lifestyle. The unique thing about prayer warriors is they practice a discipline in communicating with God that is uncommon to the community in which they minister. These individuals are noted and lauded for their special powers in God. Sometimes this causes people to hinder their growth toward maturity by refusing to communicate with the Father in fear of being inadequate in prayer. However, they would rather petition a prayer warrior to go to God on their behalf so that their prayers can be answered! This concept is creating turmoil in today's church in relationship to believers growing and gaining confidence in their own relationship with God. Therefore, we must examine intercession in the believer in order to identify basic stages of development within prayer warriors.

Typically, intercessors are identified by their physical age. Often the seniors in the church are looked to as "intercessors." Intercession should first and foremost be recognized by the discipline that is carried. Looking at various examples in the Bible provides a diversity of age in regards of intercessors. In the Book of Daniel, we can take note of Daniel and Shadrach, Meshach, and Abednego. All of these young men practiced a discipline in their youth that was uncommon amongst their peers. However, the Book of Samuel shows us that there were devout older men like the priest Eli who mentored Samuel, a child. The mentorship of Samuel afforded him a tutor who understood a methodology of hearing God's voice. In the making of a prayer warrior, it is not uncommon for someone to have others who played important roles of implementing prayer in their lives. Prayer is a spiritual gift that develops within the life of a person. The earlier that learners initiate their prayer lives, the longer it has to grow and be groomed within them.

The earlier we embrace a life of prayer, the more apt we become able to understand and war in spiritual battles.

Demonology is an area in the kingdom of God that is ridiculed, manipulated, and pampered. Hollywood has distorted our religious perspective of gods, demons, and spirits. We have adopted a skeptical view of our interaction with them. Many in the church of the living God walk in fear of gods, demons, and spirits because they lack tangible knowledge of how to recognize them and how demonic forces affect their lives. It is quite challenging for individuals to identify negative influences in their lives when they are operating in the traditions of their community.

The traditions of our community are the mannerisms, daily actions, conversations, and the like. However, when we are consumed by our communities, it makes it difficult for us to recognize ill behaviors and thoughts and make our own decisions. Satan desires that the believers not show any productivity and peace of mind. Prayer is an arsenal against demonic activity.

Chapter 2

GENDERS IN PRAYER

T HE PRACTICE OF intercession is becoming increasingly dominated by women. Though this creates a gender divide in intercessory teams, women dominating the prayer field are correcting the misconception that only men, and especially those in leadership, are adequate for intercession. Men are not absent from nor are they blind to need for prayer. Women who pray are just as needed as men who pray. Today, because of a gender-based society, men and women are challenged with who is positioned to talk to God as in roles and responsibility. The truth is Jesus validates both genders to seek the Father. Fortunate for the body of Christ, the intercessor is not identified by gender but is validated by maturity and justified through Christ.

Intercession is done in respect to the kingdom of God. Intercessors provide assistance in managing, establishing, and the maintaining of God's kingdom through the governing of prayer. Intercession originated with the Father and is continued through us "Kingdom Kids." The intercessors' origin was with the creation of man. Isaiah writes in chapter 59, verse 16: "And he saw that there was no man, and wondered that there was no intercessor: therefore his arm brought salvation unto him; and his righteousness, it sustained him." This illustrates the concern and need for an intercessor. The qualities of an intercessor help every believer aid in the work of the Holy Spirit.

Our qualities are justified by our character. Characteristics of a modern-day intercessor are as follows: communes with God daily, possesses a heavenly dialect, lives in worship to God, offers praise, and exhibits integrity to prayer and meditation. The intercessor is a person who could very easily be you!

The character of an intercessor is not predicated on their socioeconomic status. An intercessor can easily be identified by the disciplines they practice. Devotion to learning the Word of God and practicing godly principles are basic traits of a prayer warrior. Learning the Word of God will enable them to engage in intercession because it will empower them to understand the movements of God in affirmation of the Spirit of God in them.

Confidentiality is an important trait that intercessors must possess. Intercessors are not the media, and it is not their job to exploit their fellow sisters and brothers for selfish gain, self-will, or directing who they are to become. More so, it is always their purpose to expose demonic plans that are set for the destruction of God's missions and visions for the progression of His kingdom. Intercessors are not instigators nor are they investigators for self-interest. However, there are many systems that use the gift of the intercessor to manipulate people and to dominate them.

The intercessor must be available to the leadership of the church or organization to aid and encourage the spiritual growth, maintenance, and stability of the ministry. Intercessors must have a daily devotion with God. "We must never wait until we feel like praying before we pray for others. Prayer is like any other work; we may not feel like working, but once we have been at it for a bit, we begin to feel like working."[1] This daily devotion is time set aside for communion with the Father. If you don't employ yourself to communicate with the Father, then how are you supposed to build the relationship with Him? Daily communion is necessary in the life of a prayer warrior.

Prayer warriors experience daily challenges like any other person. Being a strong person of prayer does not mean that you don't have downhearted days. Prayer is further developed through our perseverance through trials. The outcomes from prayer are limitless. Authentic prayer to God can cause unlimited breakthroughs. God is never limited by human circumstance and/or condition. Just because something does not happen does not mean that God has not heard or lacks ability in His response.

with the petition made in prayer. It will display a sign of faith towards what we have petitioned. We direct God to our petitions by contacting Him with praise. Using praise as a bond encourages us to focus on more than the outward expression of our faith. We must believe that we have sent Jesus first on our behalf regarding our petition.

Deuteronomy 33:7 cries out for four blessings for Judah, which are as follows:

1. The Lord to hear the voice of Judah
2. Judah to be brought unto his people
3. Judah's hands to be sufficient to defend himself
4. The Lord to help him against his enemies

Recognizing the fruit of these blessings allows us to see the power of the Lion of Judah (Christ). In Revelation 5:5 it states that only the Lion of the tribe of Judah prevailed to open the book and loose the seven seals. Therefore, when we engage in our intercession, we are employing Christ, the one who has the keys to every door. Because His voice triumphed to be heard by the Father, it assures us that the fragrance of our petitions will reach the nostrils of the Father. Revelation 5:8 tells us that the heavenly elders fell down before the Lamb. After Christ, Judah, the Lamb, took the book that no man could open, with praise and worship He offered the vials filled with odors, which are the prayers of saints. Hebrews 7:14 confirms that Christ sprang out of Judah.

Since we are made in the image of the Father, the Son, and the Holy Spirit, we are able to perform like Judah. When we have communed with the Father and our confidence is in Him, we are to praise Him outwardly and openly because He has heard our prayers and we have faith in Him to perform His will.

David is a perfect example of what a "Judah-ist" would look like (a praiser). Praise affirms our prayers! Praise disciplines our spirit and commands our flesh to acknowledge God in all of our ways. Every prayer warrior of God must have some level of outward expression for God. "Celebration is at the heart of the way of Christ."[2]

Prayer warriors who praise God strengthen and verify their faith in God. It must be understood that it is possible to praise God without possessing a belief in God. It is possible to praise God without worshipping God. The phrase from Psalm 150:6: "Let everything that has breath praise the LORD" (NKJV) is commonly quoted in church. Some don't understand that praise alone does not validate a relationship with God. If there is no relationship with God, then there is no power. It is credible to note that all of God's children possess a measure of His power. Many have a hesitation in tapping into our internal power—the power that God has granted His children. This upsets the enemy because God strengthens the believer beyond our own outward expressions.

Worship validates the existence of our God. "Worship is our response to the overtures of love from the heart of the Father. Its central reality is found in spirit and truth."[3] No individual can become a prayer warrior of the Most High and not possess a passion to worship God the Creator. Worship is a prerequisite to entering into the most holy place.

Jesus told Satan, "Thou shalt worship the Lord thy God, and him only shalt thou serve" (Luke 4:8). Satan understands worship because he has angels and servants that worship him. However, Satan's knowledge is limited because he cannot comprehend how believers can worship the Lord God after all of the *hell* (turmoil) he (Satan) puts them through.

Prayer warriors who have intense worship lifestyles are usually people who have weathered storms greater than most of their age, peers, family, and/or community. Worship not only assists the prayer warrior in day-to-day survival, but it also releases them from anxiety while waiting on the manifestation of their petition. Matthew, chapter 4, verses 10 and 11, tell us after Jesus chastened the devil concerning worshipping the true and living God, the devil fled. Does worship exist in your life? Worship is not a waste of time but is a beneficial practice and should be practiced by every intercessor.

Finally, in managing our prayer lives, we must always put James 4:7 to practice because, every time you think of the Father, temptation will be present to draw you away from Him. Satan knows if he can get the attention of your flesh "by any means necessary," then you've afforded him the opportunity to distract you from the voice of God because you're busy acting out of your flesh. As intercessors, we must seize more and more of God and His disciplines. This is the path of maturity. Intercessors must stay in constant communion with God. All answers, solutions, principles, procedures, businesses ideas, inventions, and knowledge lie at the door of intercession. Without intercession, we lack everything.

Chapter 4

INTERCESSION IN YOU

WHAT IS THE definition of intercession? According to Webster, *intercession* means an entreaty in favor of another or mediation in a dispute.[1] Both of these definitions depict the effect of intercession from God's perspective. God knew, in order for man to take dominion over the earth, that he would need someone who would intercede or entreat on his behalf. God knew that the soul of man was not stable enough to walk in dominion in the earth, so He made provision for His Spirit to govern the soul of man. God knew that if His Spirit would govern man, the Spirit would make intercession for man's soul. God knew this would be needed because of the temptations of man's flesh. Without the presence of God's Spirit, man would likely yield his soul to Satan because of the weakness of his flesh. God's Spirit lives in our soul, but the condition of our soul dictates the liberty of God's Spirit.

Theoretically, our soul operates as the house for God. God said in Isaiah 56:7 that His house will be called a *house of prayer*. The intercessor and intercession is woven together by the thread of the Holy Spirit to make intercession effective. *Prayer is not difficult!*

It is important to understand the beginnings of the

earth. God has always been interested in being heard. When we look at how He spoke everything into existence and then life into the beings He created, we see the significance and power in His commands. Just imagine the residue of power that was left inside us! As we look at the creation story, it is amazing how that which was without form and void (Gen. 1:2), the essence of nothing, was able to hear the voice of God. Romans 8:29 tells us, "For whom he did foreknow, he also did predestinate to be conformed to the image of his Son, that he might be the firstborn among many brethren." If we were foreknown and predestinated to be conformed to the image of His Son, then we bear a divine impartation that enables us to hear Him impeccably.

The relationship of a prayer warrior to the Spirit gives the ability to hear and discern beyond trials and problems. Prayer warriors are not free of trouble or trials; however, a prayer warrior has the ability to search for the inner strength of God as a force to overcome outward conflict. Practicing prayer is not a sign of weakness. In order for us to remain strong, we must learn not to depend on our own abilities. Recognizing our own inabilities and our need to trust in God's complete capabilities is the beginning of building a life of prayer dependent on God as the source.

Chapter 5

THE ECHELONS OF PRAYER

W E CAN PARALLEL the progress as we mature in intercession to the progression through the sections of the tabernacle. The Old Testament tabernacle was divided into three sections: the outer court, the inner court, and the most holy place. As we develop a mature prayer life, God continues to use this method for His children longing to get close to Him. Entering into the most holy place comes with training and experience. This training should come from our pastor; however, this is not always the case.

There is a controversial teaching in the body of Christ that, regardless of training, anyone who wants is capable of going deeply into the spirit realm and engaging in spiritual hermeneutics. In every other religion, it is understood and respected that training must take place before delving into the depths of that religion. I am not stating that we must be trained to talk to God, but I am saying that there are distinct disciplines that must be possessed when longing to know the heartbeat of God. Once we are trained with the necessary disciplines, then we will eventually be granted access into the depths of God. The spirit realm is endless. We will never reach a dead end in regards to prayer. It would be inaccurate to present the Spirit of God as a single level. A reward to those that diligently seek the Lord (Heb. 11:6) is to permit them to travel into the depths of who He is.

OUTER COURT

In the outer court, every believer has right to engage in prayer. This level of prayer is not contingent upon maturity in the gospel. Intercessors commune with God about life, day to day issues, family members, circumstances, etc. Typically, intercessors look for external appearances of God to affirm their faith in God and His ability to answer their prayers. Outer court intercessors do commune with God, but very seldom do they wait and listen for a response. Outer court intercession can be imitated!

INNER COURT

The next level of intercession is the called the inner court. In the inner court, prayer is activated mostly in these arenas: church services, prayer meetings, and other similar events. Intercessors commune with God for His blessings about an event, situations, burdens, service, etc. These look very similar to outer court intercessors; however, these intercessors have the ability to praise God yet lack belief. It is common for them to look good outwardly but carry serious doubt, confusion, and disbelief about what they have petitioned unto God. This is a popular place. Many people desire this place because it can be imitated, and it provides them an opportunity to be seen by men.

MOST HOLY PLACE

Intercessors at this level must be mature in the Word of the God. They can gain access to the most holy things. They commune with God about the building of His kingdom. They seek God for principles, understanding, correction, etc., for ministry, communities, and personal edification. In the most holy place of prayer, believers are able to hear *rhema* words from God and feed on them. It is twice that Jesus speaks about food for the soul (Matt. 4:4; Luke 4:4). Yes, the written Word is food at all three levels, but only intercessors in the most holy place can eat of Him from words from prayer. *God still speaks!*

It is common for these intercessors to go unnoticed and unrecognized. They seek no personal glory. They are cautious when delivering a message from the Lord. They are careful about verbiage, timing, and personal acknowledgment for God's words. These individuals bear dreams and revelations.

Permission is not determined by a natural title or position. Permission is granted with maturity. God checks the accountability of our relationship with Him. A leader can affirm us in this place but the leader and the believer are both held accountable if the individual is not mature enough to hold the keys of the most holy place. The accountability to God for intercessors of the most holy place is great and can even be life threatening. *This cannot be imitated!* The Spirit of God that lies in every believer confirms evidence of this place. Only in the most holy place of prayer can you progress, going from glory to glory (2 Cor. 3:18). This level of intercession is endless.

Consequences

Outer court

The outer court is usually occupied by baby Christians, "new births." God knows that they are just getting to know Him, and He is lenient.

Inner court

The inner court is occupied by laity and leaders. Also, wavering Christians hang out here. The consequences of this place are more severe because, typically, everyone that lingers here is committed to ministry either inside or outside of the four walls of an assembly. These believers are not new to dating God; during their relationship, He has given them insight because He loves them. However, they fail to realize the closer that they come to the glory, the more accountable God holds them.

Most holy place

The most holy place is occupied by five-fold ministry gifts (Eph. 4:11), those who have been set apart because of their diligence in prayer (prayer warriors), Jesus, etc. The consequences of this place are most severe because of the accountability to God.

Yes, all three phases have accountability to God. However, after entering into the holy place, we become privileged in knowing more about the heart and mind of God. For this reason, our chastening can be stern. It is in this place that the privileges God grants to the prayer warrior, if misused, can result in the consequence of withholding the glory.

Chapter 6

CODE OF CONDUCT

Matthew 6:1–18

I N THE CODE of conduct for interceding, Jesus teaches us how to address the Father by petitioning Him through prayer. There are several areas we must acknowledge when engaging in prayer according to Jesus' instructions. The disciples wanted to know how to pray. In Matthew 6:9–13, Jesus provided a model prayer while exemplifying the elements of a complete prayer. The elements are perspectives of God. For example, the first element is to acknowledge that we are talking to the God, the Most High. As we develop our prayer lives, we must condition ourselves by practicing the art of communicating with the Father.

Our Father which art in heaven, Hallowed be thy name.

- Always recognize our Father, God, the greatest deity known!
- Acknowledge, proclaim, and announce how infallible He is.

21

Thy kingdom come, Thy will be done in earth, as it is in heaven.

- No matter what we are petitioning to God, we know who He is, and His Son has already died for this cause.
- Petition for agreement between heaven and earth (God's will).

Give us this day our daily bread

- We ask Him to fill our space with His presence, His words, and His peace in our souls, which is our daily food. We know this because of our daily communion (Matt. 4:4; Luke 4:4).

And forgive us our debts, as we forgive our debtors.

- We need God to forgive us because we don't want unforgiveness to hinder the answers to our prayers or petitions (Matt. 6:14–15).

And lead us not into temptation, but deliver us from evil: For thine is the kingdom, and the power, and the glory, for ever. Amen

- We ask God to deliver us from the lusts of our flesh for, in His kingdom, all power and glory belongs to Him forever.
- We realize that our own will could be initiating our prayer. However, we don't want our will, but His will, to be done.

MATTHEW 6:14-18

For if ye forgive men their trespasses, your heavenly Father will also forgive you.

- We ask the Father to help us walk in forgiveness because, as we forgive others, He will forgive us, and this will free Him to respond to our prayers.

But if ye forgive not men their trespasses, neither will your Father forgive your trespasses.

- Unforgiveness will annul our prayer or petition.

Moreover when ye fast, be not, as the hypocrites, of a sad countenance: for they disfigure their faces, that they may appear unto men to fast. Verily I say unto you, They have their reward.

- We mustn't make a covenant with God for vain and selfish glory.

But thou, when thou fastest, anoint thine head, and wash thy face; That thou appear not unto men to fast, but unto thy Father which is in secret: and thy Father, which seeth in secret, shall reward thee openly.

- Intercessors must be mature and not seeking or longing for affirmation from men. Affirmation must be in our souls as we are connected with Father.

BIBLIOGRAPHY

Attridge, Harold W., ed. *The HarperCollins Study Bible New Revised Standard Version: Student Edition*. New York: HarperOne, 1989.

Campbell, Ben. *Hearing God's Call*. Grand Rapids, MI: William B. Eerdmans, 2002.

Day, J. Daniel. *Seeking the Face of God*. Macon, GA: Nurturing Faith, 2013.

Foster, Richard. *Celebration of Discipline*. New York: Harper & Row, 1978.

Webster's Dictionary for Students Special Encyclopedic Ed. Darien, CT: Federal Street Press, 2007.

Yoder, John Howard. *Body Politics*. Nashville: 1992.

NOTES

INTRODUCTION

1. Richard Foster, *Celebration of Discipline* (New York: Harper & Row, 1978).

2. J. Daniel Day, *Seeking the Face of God* (Macon, GA: Nurturing Faith, 2013).

3. *Webster's Dictionary for Students Special Encyclopedic Ed.* (Darien, CT: Federal Street Press, 2007), s.v. "prayer."

4. *Webster's*, s.v. "accountable."

5. Foster, *Celebration of Discipline.*

6. Harold W. Attridge, ed., *The HarperCollins Study Bible* (New York: HarperOne, 1989).

7. Foster, *Celebration of Discipline.*

8. Attridge, *The HarperCollins Study Bible.*

9. Foster, *Celebration of Discipline.*

CHAPTER 2
GENDERS IN PRAYER

1. Foster, *Celebration of Discipline.*

CHAPTER 3
THE PERSONALITY OF A PRAYER WARRIOR

1. Attridge, *The HarperCollins Study Bible.*

2. Foster, *Celebration of Discipline.*

3. Ibid.

CHAPTER 4
INTERCESSION IN YOU

1. *Webster's*, s.v. "intercession."

ABOUT THE AUTHOR

ROOSEVELT ETHRIDGE IS a trusted Generation X voice at the forefront of international ministry. Pastor of Living Word International Ministries in Wilson, NC, he serves as overseer of Intersecting Ministries, an umbrella of Living Word Ministries International. Globally, Overseer Ethridge serves as general overseer of River of Life Christian Church in Cagayan De Oro City, Philippines; MDOC Global Fellowship, Inc., Cagayan De Oro City, Philippines; and Ebenezer Iglesias in Naples, Italy. Overseer Ethridge is international advisor for Jesus for All Nations and Network International, Inc.; CMC Network, Inc.; and Lamp Foundation International, Inc., based out of the Philippines.

His zeal and compassion for God's people have led him to reach out to the underserved and unapproachable. Overseer Ethridge's primary focus is sharing the fundamentals of the Christian faith around the globe in simple language to prepare Christians to become disciples of Jesus Christ.

He is heard each week on the Pastors Round Table on WIDU Radio. He has authored two books, including *Navigating from a Broken Place: A Life Map for Love, Relationship, and Singleness.* Overseer Ethridge is proudest to father Roosevelt Amir-Rasheed Ethridge, III, whom he raises in the fear and knowledge of the Lord while equipping him to fulfill the destiny set before him.

Follow Overseer Ethridge at @EROEU on Twitter and on the web at www.reliveglobal.org.

CONTACT THE AUTHOR

Email Address: reliveglobal@gmail.com

Web Address: www.reliveglobal.org

Facebook: Roosevelt Ethridge

Twitter: @EROEU